BOOK ANALYSIS

Written by Delphine Leloup
Translated by Emma Lunt

AF131379

The Royal Game

BY STEFAN ZWEIG

STEFAN ZWEIG

AUSTRIAN WRITER, PLAYWRIGHT, JOURNA-
LIST AND BIOGRAPHER

- **Born in Vienna in 1881**
- **Died in Brazil in 1942**
- **Notable works:**
  - *Confusion of Feelings* (1926), novella
  - *Twenty-Four Hours in the Life of a Woman* (1934), novella
  - *The Royal Game* (1943), novella

Stefan Zweig was born in Vienna, Austria in 1881, to an upper-class Jewish family. Very early on, he demonstrated a passion for everything related to art, poetry, literature and theatre. During his studies and his many travels around the world, he developed a profoundly humanistic side as well as an attachment to European culture. He became close to great writers such as Rilke, Emile Verhaeren, Romain Rolland and Jules Romain. He was passionate and terribly sensitive, and so was traumatised by the two world wars. In 1933, his books were publicly burnt in Munich. In 1942, he committed suicide in Brazil, after fleeing Europe several years previously.

THE ROYAL GAME

HUMAN NATURE AND PSYCHOLOGY

- **Genre:** novella
- **Reference edition:** Zweig, S. (2007) *The Royal Game*. Trans. Huebsch, B. W. London: Pushkin Press.
- **First edition:** 1943
- **Themes:** insanity, passion, solitude, game, sequestration

The Royal Game is a novella that was written in 1941 (and published posthumously in 1943) and is the last novella written by Stefan Zweig. It tackles many important topics such as insanity, violent passion, solitude and opposition in the face of enemy forces (which of course alludes to the rise of totalitarianism that struck Europe during the end of the 1930s). Zweig's writing focuses heavily on analysing human psychology and nature. The author later confessed to his first wife Friderike that he was inspired to compose this novella by his own passion for chess.

SUMMARY

The novella was not originally divided into different sections.

PART I

The story begins on a cruise liner when the narrator, whose name is unknown, casts his eyes upon a group of journalists who seem to be interviewing a young man. It is the famous chess champion, Mirko Czentovic.

He is described at length as an idiotic man, although gifted with a great capacity for concentration and observation when he practices his 'art'. As an orphan, he was taken in when he was a child by the charitable village pastor who tried, in vain, to provide him with an intellectual education. Mirko failed at everything, but lifted himself out of laziness at the sight of a chessboard. Introduced to numerous more experienced players, he won games and progressed until he gained the respect of the most renowned competitors.

PART II

The narrator, who desperately wants to meet him and put his talent to the test, elaborates a plan to force Czentovic to play a game in public. As the best way of attracting his attention is by simply playing chess, he decides to introduce chess evenings. His initiative quickly attracts the curious including McConnor, a rich businessman who is full of himself. They compete against each other and the latter loses.

Czentovic himself witnesses the scene and shows contempt for the two opponents, which annoys McConnor. Furthermore, the champion does not want to begin a chess game without remuneration. Consequently, a large sum of money is offered to him for his participation in a tournament the following day.

Punctually the following day, Czentovic faces his opponent, McConnor, as planned. He manages to reduce his strategy to nothing in only a few moves. Soon after, the businessman goes one further: he wants revenge! During the equally short second game, a mysterious passenger helps him to draw against Czentovic. Humiliated, the latter demands a new game against the unknown man the next day. Given the responsibility of persuading the man to do battle against the grand master a second time, the narrator leaves to find him.

PART III

Hidden in the shadows, on the deck, the enigmatic passenger seems happy to be approached by the narrator. After having agreed to accept the challenge set by Czentovic, Dr B decides to tell his story and the reasons that drove him to be so passionate about chess.

The former lawyer was imprisoned, long ago, by the Gestapo because he had helped to hide the riches of the Austrian imperial family and other great nobility. But Hitler wanted to get his hands on the goods belonging to the richest people and proceeded to make many arrests. Dr B was locked up for four months in a hotel room with no way of knowing what was happening outside. He was regularly interrogated by the militia and very quickly showed signs of insanity due to his solitude.

One day, while he was being interrogated, he saw a book in the coat pocket of one of the officers and managed to steal it. It was a manual detailing the techniques of the best chess players in the world. He learnt it down to the last word. He then imagined his own chess games and became so obsessed by this new occupation that he became schizophrenic. On his release, he promised himself to never again touch a chessboard.

PART IV

Honouring the engagement he had made the day before, Dr B arrives at the competition, which is taking place in the smoking room, and begins the first game feeling a little unsure of himself. However, he wins! The second game also seems promising. However, Dr B's behaviour changes completely and he quivers with tics and rictus (which is nothing other than a manifestation of his insanity). Losing all control and becoming delirious, he is forced by the narrator to stop the game. The book ends with Czentovic congratulating his brilliant opponent.

CHARACTER STUDY

We do not know his first name nor his age. However, we know that he is Austrian and that he boarded the liner with a friend. He is the narrator (although he gives the floor to Dr B when he tells his story) and also an important character in the novella.

He seems quite curious by nature and knows how to use strategy and manipulation to get what he wants. Subconsciously, he wants to be the man to knock down the "hero" Czentovic, but he is only the person that initiates the first chess game. An active challenger at the start of the novella, he progressively gets away from the action to become only a passive spectator of the game.

He describes himself as an intellectual and looks down on men that he sees as inferior due to their stupidity (Czentovic) or their lack of public-spiritedness (McConnor). He is very patient and lends an ear to the problems of others (he gives up his time for Dr B when he expresses his wish to tell him his story). Rather loyal in friendship and very obliging, he tries to bring his new companion back to reason when he notices that he is, as in the past, getting carried away by the frenzy of the game to the point of losing control of himself.

This character is the only one that plays chess for pleasure. He does not play for money (unlike Czentovic), nor as a means of survival (unlike Dr B) and there is no chance of letting his bad character or frustration explode.

The description of this scholarly man strangely makes us think of Stefan Zweig himself. In the prologue of his work, the author announces that he had got hold of a little chess manual and that this purchase had inspired the theme of his novella. Similarly to Zweig who was outraged by the Nazi regime before escaping it, the narrator witnesses a war of groups. The battle between the Croatian strategist and the Austrian thinker seems to be a metaphor of those that opposed the European intellectuals during the rise of totalitarianism.

MIRKO CZENTOVIC

His childhood was very unhappy. The son of a Croatian boatman, he found himself orphaned when his father disappeared at sea. He was 12 years old.

Czentovic does not seem to be someone who is fundamentally intelligent. He is simple-minded and had trouble retaining lessons as a child. Reflecting and calmly giving his opinion are difficult things for him, which seriously tarnishes his reputation. In the past, his tutor, the village pastor, described him to his friends as a very docile child who did not object to chores, but he did, however, reproach his lack of initiative:

> "Whatever he was told to do he did: fetched water, split wood, worked in the field, washed up the kitchen, and he could be relied upon to execute - even if with exasperating slowness - every service that was demanded. But what

grieved the kindly pastor most about the blockhead was his total lack of co-operation. He performed no deed unless specially directed, asked no questions, never played with other lads, and sought no occupation of his own accord; after Mirko had concluded his work about the house, he would sit idly with that empty stare one sees with grazing sheep, without participating in the slightest in what might be going on" p. 3.

Surrounded by adults, Mirko clearly had trouble fitting in and was very withdrawn. Furthermore, his delay compared to children of his age seemed impossible to fill. At twenty years old, he still did not know how to write properly in his own language nor even to count without using his fingers. Thus, his success in the world of chess was, for him, a lifeline to cling to in order to make his place in the world. He considers his pastime as the best there is. Pretentious and corrupt, money is more of a motivation for him than the true passion for the game. Thus he only plays for money.

In the book, Mirko's form of intelligence is opposed to that of Dr B, who is truly fascinated by the game. His strength relies on good observation and the speed of action. While he is depicted as being mentally deficient from the start of the story, Czentovic is gradually redeemed in the novella as his behaviour seems normal compared to Dr B. Also, while we see him as a social climber and pretentious from the start of the story, in the last lines, he comes down off his pedestal and swallows his pride to congratulate his opponent on his good knowledge of chess.

Physically, he has a large forehead, a "peasant head" and is blond and well-built. He has drooping eyelids and a purple face.

MCCONNOR

Having started from nothing, this Scottish man prides himself on having succeeded professionally and flashes his money in an ostentatious manner. He used to be an engineer and worked in the oil wells in California.

He is, although he does not realise it, the narrator's puppet (when he suggests to him to go to great lengths to organise a tournament). This very pretentious character deals badly with defeat and never lets go. He uses his fortune as bait to get what he wants (namely the chess game against the world champion). His ambition and aggression are infectious.

He is described as stocky with wide shoulders, a square jaw and solid teeth. His appearance is quite athletic. His yellowish colouring is due to his love for whisky.

DR B

Dr B is undoubtedly the most important character in the book and it is his life that is explained in the most detail. He also competes against the world chess leader: Mirko Czentovic. He was apparently a lawyer or solicitor before his arrest. This character is quite ambivalent in terms of behaviour and shows different attitudes according to whether he is in full monomania or not (the act of focusing his spirit on a fixed and repetitive idea). He admits to having often played chess against himself in prison by using the black and white pawns one after the other. Dr B is therefore a victim of having his thoughts and conscience split in two. This mental deviance could be one of the symptoms of schizophrenia. Nevertheless, this term is never used as such in the book.

He is calm and poised when he is not subjected to his addiction to the game. He is rational, carefully analysing situations and showing tact and courtesy towards others players. He is a scholarly man (just like the narrator). He is altruistic and loves to help others out. He is also a man of honour as he refused any collaboration with the Gestapo to protect his former clients.

He demonstrates modesty by stating that he has not touched a chessboard for 25 years, despite the fact that he defeated the world champion. He is not nervous when he plays and his calmness during the first chess game that he wins against Czentovic contrasts with the fury that overwhelms him during the second game. He is actually struck by insanity upon seeing a chessboard. His violent passion for chess overrides his reasoning and finishes him off. Indeed, he attempted to throw himself from the window of the prison during his incarceration. While he held his opponent in high regard during the first game, he shoots him a death glare during the second game and becomes very scornful of him. He is aggressive and sensitive when he thinks that Mirko is trying to destroy his game by slowing the speed of his moves. His anguish manifests itself in tics and spasms.

Physically, he is described like a ghost: he is white, and has a thin and angular face. His age is presumed to be 45.

While the narrator seems to have numerous things in common with Stefan Zweig, we could say the same about Dr B. Like him, Zweig had faced exile and left Austria. His character opposes that of Czentovic.

ANALYSIS

THE CIRCUMSTANCES SURROUNDING THE RISE OF NAZISM IN THE 20TH CENTURY

The day after the First World War, Germany, the great loser of the conflict, faced a true economic, political and social nightmare. Following the decisions imposed during the Treaty of Versailles, Germany was weighed down by the financial debt that it had established with the victorious nations and suffered from inflation. This instability was the breeding ground for the demands of Adolf Hitler, a national socialist. Denouncing the humiliation suffered by his people, he decided to make his image the symbol of Germany and, quickly, he made Berlin a large cultural centre filled with art and patriotic propaganda. In the wake of this, he made military service obligatory, created an air army (the *Luftwaffe*) and ordered the construction of submarines to attack enemies who oppressed their country. In 1934, he was officially named head of state. In 1938, the German chancellor annexed Austria: the union between the two nations was called the *Anschluss*. The nationalist and fascist movement overran the German borders and found supporters throughout the whole of Europe.

Austrian and German intellectuals, who were opposed to the regime, were distressed when faced with the homo-phobic, xenophobic and criminal actions of Hitler's Nazi movement. A great number of them left their countries which had become hostile ground. While abroad they tried to come together in favour of peace and humanity. The

German authors specialised in writing historic novels where they regularly highlighted the triumph of intelligence and spirit over the cruelty and brutality of certain totalitarian regimes.

A fervent supporter of life and the human cause, Zweig sharply denounced the Nazi regime and criticised it in *The Royal Game*. One part of the book is thus dedicated to the interrogations led by the Gestapo, which resembled true torture: brutality, intimidation, deprivation of sleep, light or food, isolation, removal of time markers, etc. The incarceration, which could last several months, aimed to break the psychological balance of the detainees in order to manipulate them more easily. In the case of Dr B, even if chess kept him afloat, the trauma ended up getting the better of him and affected him considerably.

Zweig liked to gather an abundance of material before beginning to write, in order to give precise descriptions of the events and individuals. This made him a powerful conveyor of knowledge. The writer also felt doubly affected by the Nazi issue: on the one hand he was an intellectual forced into exile due to his political opinions, and on the other hand he had to flee the German Third Reich as a Jew threatened by racial persecutions.

Having lost all faith in humanity and no longer able to cope with seeing the path being taken by the European society in which he believed so much, he committed suicide in Petrópolis with his wife in 1941.

DR B AND CZENTOVIC, OPPOSING PERSONALITIES AND VALUES

The two most important protagonists in the novella are Dr B and Czentovic. As we have previously seen, these two men have distinct personalities and embody different values. While Czentovic is strategic, calculating at chess and possesses the intelligence of a robot conditioned to play the game, Dr B relies more on his reflection and ethics to foil the traps that his opponent sets for him.

The brute force and indifference of the champion, who does not mix feelings with his art, is comparable with the remorseless tactics of the Nazi movement. His actions are mechanical because he has been trained to play, and above all to win, chess games since his youth. A parallel can be drawn to the Hitler Youth whose members were conditioned to be racially hateful and dragged away to war. His ignorance in other areas embodies, for Zweig, the closed spirit of totalitarian regimes regarding humanism and culture.

The power of Dr B is not at all the same type as that of his Croatian enemy. An intellectual disappointed by life and greatly affected by the incarceration he previously suffered, he nevertheless still believes in the possibility of the victory of the man that thinks (and therefore of humanism) over the man that acts (Nazism).

The first game plays out in Dr B's favour and recognises his feats as a person capable of anticipating hostile moves. The second causes him to plunge back into the insanity of the game: the intellectual is vanquished, reflecting the European scholars who were silenced by the censorship and totalitarian regimes of the 20th century. Dr B's abandonment of the game is representative of the exile of the intelligentsia wounded by Nazism and forced into exile.

THE SYMBOLISM OF CHESS

The Royal Game is a story which gives prominence to military vocabulary. Many terms or phrases related to the war are used to describe the chess duel (diversion, defeat, opponent, battle, lever, generals, etc.). These occurrences make us think that, in the text, the chessboard is a representation of the Second World War.

This slab of wood chequered with 64 squares reminds us of the way in which the Nazis fictitiously divided Europe according to the territories that it did and did not want to annex. In a black and white way, the white pawns (representative of the strength of good and light) face the black pawns (negative symbols of darkness). Consequently, during the first chess game which sees Czentovic opposing Dr B, fate attributes the black pawns to the champion and the white to his opponent (which again reinforces the opposition of their ideologies a little more).

As in real life, when a conflict takes place, the figurines are mistreated, used and eliminated one after another (which perhaps refers to the pacts that Hitler made with certain German or Russian political parties before betraying them and wiping out their members). The word "checkmate" announces the end of the game and the defeat of one of the opponents through the death of his king (the Treaty of Versailles after the First World War and the conferences of the Allies, at the end of the Second World War, can be seen as the loss of a nation's power and its being divided between the great victorious powers).

FURTHER REFLECTION

SOME QUESTIONS TO THINK ABOUT...

- What are the overarching themes developed in this novella by Stefan Zweig? Can we find these same themes in his other works?
- Which literary movement would you associate with Stefan Zweig or to which writer would you compare him? Provide an argument for your answer.
- Zweig, born in 1881 to a family of Jewish Austrians, lived through the Second World War and was outraged by the Nazi regime. Establish a link between his life and both the role of the narrator of The Royal Game and the life of Dr B.
- What could the chessboard symbolise?
- Compare the characters of Dr B and Czentovic. What do they represent respectively if we think about the context of the Second World War?
- Dr B finally loses his game of chess. What do you think this defeat symbolises?
- Stefan Zweig wrote a great number of novellas. Why do you think he used this type of story that is much shorter than a novel?
- Compare the novella The Royal Game with the film adaptation by Gerd Osward in 1960. Is the director loyal to Zweig's work or does he allow himself some liberties? Explain your answer.

We want to hear from you!
Leave a comment on your online library
and share your favourite books on social media!

FURTHER READING

REFERENCE EDITION

- Zweig, S. (2007) *The Royal Game*. Trans. Huebsch, B. W. London: Pushkin Press.

REFERENCE STUDIES

- Calais, É and Roux, P. (1993) *Précis des littératures de la communauté européenne*. Bruxelles: Labor.
- Durand, A. (2016) *Le Jouer d'échecs*. Comptoir Littéraire. [Online]. [Accessed 24 September 2010]. Available from: <http://www.comptoirlitteraire.com/z.html>
- Pedagogie 2. (2016) *Stefan Zweig*, Le Joueur d'échecs. [Online]. [Accessed 26 September 2016]. Available from: <http://pedagogie2.ac-reunion.fr/lettres/tl/Vero_Zweig/plan.html>

ADAPTATIONS

- *The Royal Game*. (1960) [Film]. Gerd Oswald. Dir. West Germany: Roxy Film.

MORE FROM BRIGHTSUMMARIES.COM

- Reading guide – *Confusion of Feelings* by Stefan Zweig
- Reading guide – *Twenty-Four Hours in the Life of a Woman* by Stefan Zweig

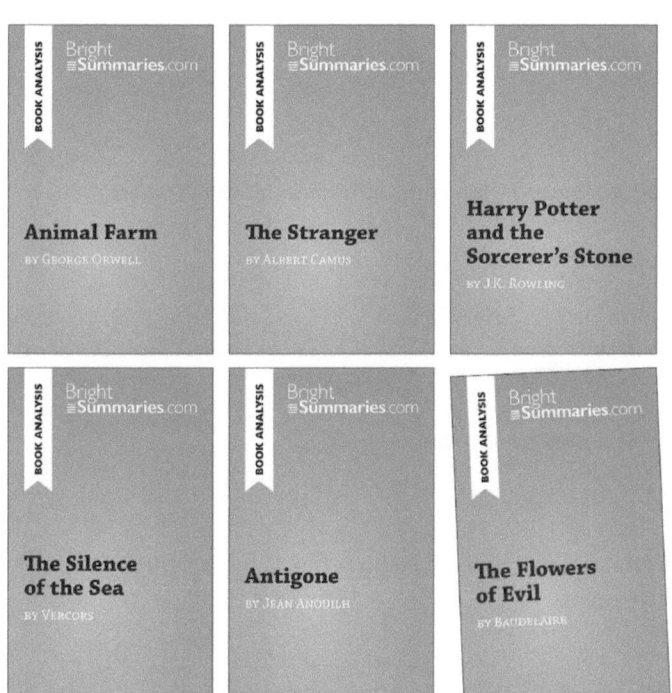